Blood Alluvium
S. Preston Duncan

Parlyaree Press
Atlanta, Georgia
www.parlyaree.com

Copyright © 2024 by S. Preston Duncan
All Rights Reserved
Printed in the United States of America
First Edition, 2024

All rights reserved. This book or any portion thereof may not be reproduced or used in any manner whatsoever without the express written permission of the publisher except for the use of brief quotations in a book review. Selections of this book have previously appeared in various literary journals and online publications as noted within the Acknowledgments.

Library of Congress Cataloging-in-Publication Data
Names: Duncan, S. Preston, Author
Title: Blood Alluvium | S. Preston Duncan
Description: First Edition | Atlanta : Parlyaree Press, 2024
Identifiers: LCCN: 2024907443 | ISBN: 978-1-961206-09-0
Subjects: LCGFT: Poetry

Design by Parlyaree Press.
Hand Illustration by Faith Anne Butler.

Blood Alluvium was designed and typefaced with Adobe Garamond Pro. Drawn in 1989 by Robert Slimbach, it is a careful, modern interpretation influenced by specimens of Garamond's original type.

Print ISBN: 978-1-961206-09-0
Ebook ISBN: 978-1-961206-10-6

For Maeve

ACCLAIM FOR
BLOOD ALLUVIUM

In this achingly lyric debut full-length collection, Duncan tackles no less than creation, God, grief, death & what follows with a poignancy that keeps the reader turning pages, swallowing poems like pomegranate seeds, one after the next. Deeply layered images carry us into the stream where memory and vision merge, where "thunder is pulled off the world like a sheet from fitful dreaming." With a lens of disparate mythologies, Duncan, like any good ferryman, brings us through the bitter to faith and sometimes back again, leaving us loath that the journey be over. ("And yet, /says the river, And yet.")

Joanna S. Lee
Author of Dissections (Finishing Line Press, 2017)
Poet Laureate of Richmond, Virginia

If you're ever worried that poetry is dying or already in the ground we stand on, you are obviously not reading the work of S. Preston Duncan. He can appeal to the academic and to the dishwasher. The jockey and the stall cleaner. Preston reminds us that no matter who we are, we are alive in this beautiful world and its beauty has mostly nothing to do with us.

Ryan Kent
Author of Everything Is On Fire: Selected Poetry 2014-2021
& the album Dying Comes With Age (Rare Bird Lit)
Richmond, Virginia

This debut washes against the skin, fully conscious of how language should settle after the flood, where it should place its pieces in the mouth and the ways in which it should transport the reader beyond corpus, clay, sediment and soul, all the while *lacquered with the runoff of ancestors we do not remember*. This collection has been *built to carry bodies* and if the question is do *I have the hands for it* then the answer is an absolute affirmative. A stunning debut of confidence and craft, *smooth as olives*, rich in texture, thought and text found in *the funnel between God's blind eye and the trailer park*. Read it today and keep it close at hand, in corners *kept for comfort*.

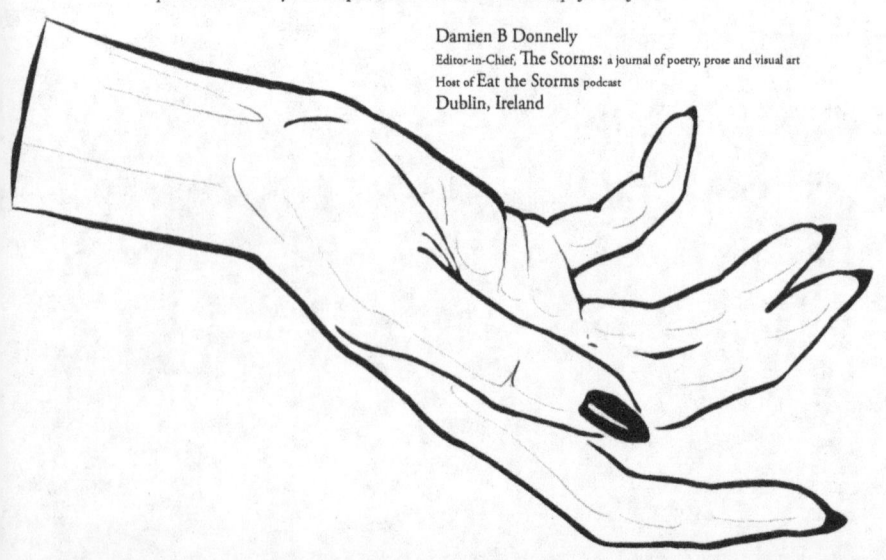

Damien B Donnelly
Editor-in-Chief, The Storms: a journal of poetry, prose and visual art
Host of Eat the Storms podcast
Dublin, Ireland

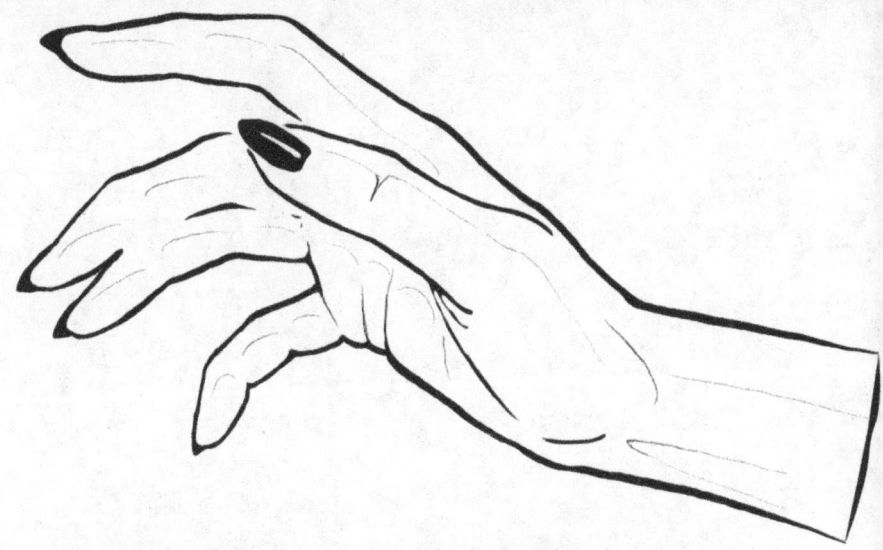

In Duncan's new collection...every poem is charged and pulses with an electric current....
Duncan's voice is full of magic and power. His imagery melds the organic and the uncanny....Yet
equally we have the specificity of concrete details coupled with these allusions, echos and symbols,
making the poems palpable and immersive....

Duncan's work is, as they said about Seamus Heaney, 'close to the earth' that is full of lush,
organic, elemental images, connected to the country, the seasons, the stars – yet transcendent too.

Described as 'a cartography of grief,' *Blood Alluvium* is deeply elegiac, fusing luminous imagery
of loss and longing....This book is both hallelujah and elegy, mourning and celebration, and as
immersive as the rising waters that swell and forbode throughout the book – the waters which
represent the passing and taking away of lives and eons....

Throughout the book, the language is dangerous and powerful - and there is an affecting and
candid expression of the vulnerability of all things 'both dog and author' are 'broken gods' and, in
a metafiction comment Duncan says himself - 'no painting is safe'.

Duncan is a visionary poet who brings to mind, with his deeply spiritual perspective and acute
understanding of the fate of the earth, W.S Merwin, and there are echos of T.S. Eliot too in the
dark incantations of some lines....

It is impossible not to be affected by the collection's emotional truths, dazzling and penetrating
imagery, and unremitting and sonorous music that runs throughout.

Some collections impact you emotionally, others leave you in awe at their craft - this collection
does both...

A stunning collection with its own unique and redemptive music.

                                            Anna Saunders
                                            CEO, Cheltenham Poetry Festival
                                            Author of *The Prohibition of Touch* (Indigo Dreams, 2022)
                                            This review appears in full at *Ink Sweat and Tears UK*

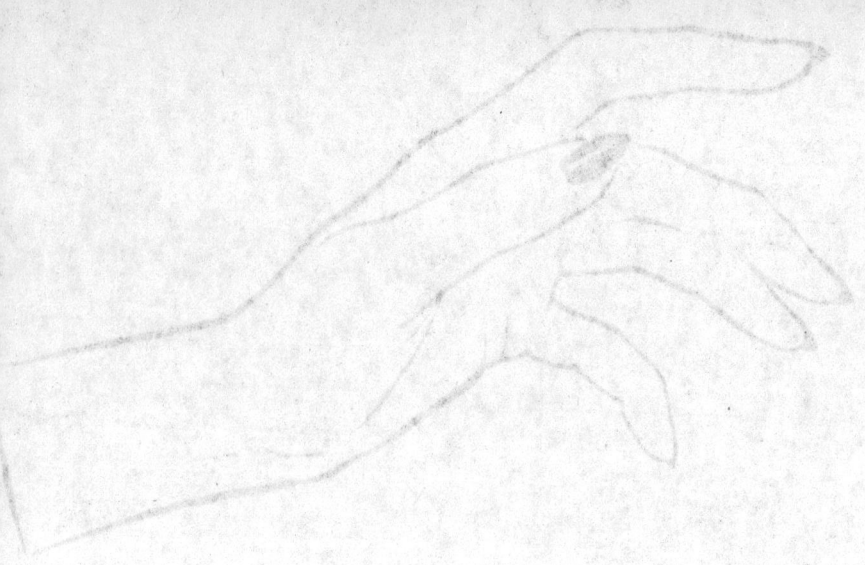

BLOOD ALLUVIUM

S. PRESTON DUNCAN

Table Of Contents

I. Effigy for the Flood
Again, We Are New — 3
Oceanography — 4
Water Below — 5
We Don't Have a Grocery Store but We Got Farmer Joe's — 6
Harvest — 7
Sky Burial — 8
What We Could Say With What We Were Given — 9
Driving Around Surry County With Drugs in the Car — 10
We Do Not Sleep Alone — 11
John Prine on a Full Moon in April — 12
You Don't Need to Know Much About Dogs
to Tell She's Thoroughbred — 13
How Short We Are — 14

II. Elegy in Pieces
A Week from which Beauty has been Erased — 19
Ba'alei Shem — 20
Our Hands Did Not Shed This Blood, Nor Did Our Eyes See — 21
Yesterday I Went Downtown — 22
Death Dresses — 23
In the Afternoon I Will Be Home — 25
Empty Road Where Someone Is Walking — 26
Don't let your cut foot ruin our walk on the beach — 27
Because Jerusalem Is a Point in My Heart I Have Fallen
Asleep With Candles Burning — 28
We Can't Help Ourselves — 29
Generation — 30
Pogroms and Shoahs — 31
The Name of Every God Is Surrounded by Loss — 32
Recipes — 33
The Well — 35
Therin — 36
The Gravel Pits — 37
Love[sic] — 38
Ad Astra — 41

III. The Cailleach
Blood Alluvium	45
In the Stillness After Impact	46
The New Weather	47
The Swallows	48
Cartography of Winter	49
You Don't Steal From the Witch's Garden	50
A Radiology of Time in Garamond	51
Tír na nÓg	52
Now That I Have Met Your Family of Ghosts, I Renounce My Nation	53
The Sound in This Time of Being	54
A Map of the Underworld	56
Sain	57
Tell Ourselves Apart	59
Initiation	60

Acknowledgments 63

I
Effigy for the Flood

I
Elegy for the Flood

Again, We Are New

The first time this happened
There was nothing to remember

Your eyes were shocked
To be eyes

Your palms
Smooth as olives
Learned the language of sunlight
Of springwater uttered
From stone

You have known this colony
Of time

How it splits the pomegranate
How these bloodied seeds
Find the river
That knew you

When we were all standing at once
In the same strange skin.

Oceanography

If we awoke to find we were once again children,
still roped up in all this newsprint,
toppling with the weight of what we have wound
in butcher paper, unable to trick back to sea

If we had been born to alkali flats in
a chant of sagebrush and dust fire,
only known water at bedtime
as a lie about God
or an autograph of starlight
in the dry, tumbling night

what would we have made
when we unfolded the earth
to find we had been misplaced?

This is the way we evaporate:
our footprints the shape of puddles,
every desert a memory of the ocean floor.

Water Below

I hang railroad spikes from the roof over the porch. She puts up windchimes that look like the sun and the moon bent out of the shed at the edge of where we lived before. At night we are the silent ones wearing paths through each other. The street throbs with bullfrogs. Everywhere the swamp arrives, I am waiting to drive a stake through it. Even now on this hill that risks everything. Tonight there were owls in the yard. I heard a generation of bald cypress forming in their throats. The muddied edge of Virginia. The wet cardboard of it. I heard all that. When the wind blows it drives the sounds away. Like a train coming apart in the air.

We Don't Have a Grocery Store but We Got Farmer Joe's

Joe wants to sell me soil.
He is in the greenhouse
with a crown of tomatoes.

When he laughs they are green skulls
roping the shoulders of an immigrant prayer.
When he stops they are tomatoes again.

Joe holds a flower pot up to his accent.
Water pours right through it.

You see? he says

And I do.

His suspenders are red and full of bargains.
In the cooler are fresh brown eggs;
they have been spinning on the tip of a chicken all day.

Time to time a tourist stops in.
They hit the gravel like sunshine
on its way across the river.

Williamsburg stretches for them in the parking lot
where bags of Joe's soil
slump against the chain link
and get a little harder to lift every year.

Harvest

was a trauma with human eyes
the color of old photographs,

clouds curdling into cherry blossoms,
a cotton wind laying across a field
of flammable powders,
a cane that had not once wobbled
turning over in the road.

At the bar a preacher
drags something ruined
across the stage
like a cigarette,
like a wheelchair;
it is plain they have come to fight.

Come back with a moustache
               and a typewriter on a small table.
With hair like demolished haystacks.
A song written in birdshot
picked from black parts of the sky.
Say *I squeezed the trigger, and then*
        insulation   *everywhere.*

Come back baled in madness,
reeking of moonlight,
a frustration of whiskey
and weekdays
that falls to the floor and demands
to be carried out.

You shouldn't have the breath to say *please*
by the time you finish explaining yourself.

Sky Burial

They weren't exactly falling from the clouds,
but if it had happened all at once
we'd have called it a storm.

We'd have been clear as an atheist's prayer,
picked them up one by one
and recited their names in our sleep.

As it happened, I carried them
to the edge of the woods
once a week or so,

laid them like flowers around the juniper,
waved my hands as though stumbling from the sky.

Their feathers in the wind
for a moment, an awakening

What We Could Say With What We Were Given

A miraculous thing happened.
We need it to happen again
or we'll make it into a religion
nobody will believe.

Go, find God.
Tell them we are cratered with opioid,
lacquered with the runoff
of ancestors we do not remember.

We are terrified of language
and the faces that appear behind it—
their consonance of jawline,
the constant vowel of their expression.

Tell them we need something
we can't wipe from our eyes.

We have imagined lifetimes of doubt
and they are unbelievable.

Driving Around Surry County With Drugs in the Car

They built this church to hoard a graveyard,
a colony of ghosts they call by Hebrew names.
The children grow up believing in angels
that are ghosts.

All the grandmothers who couldn't let go
are given a sword and some kind of new eyes.

They arrive at judgments. They fly around
with a thousand voices.

We Do Not Sleep Alone

Neighborhoods extinguish
in a wreath of dreary monuments
a stack of errant heritage

the yellow tape
the alcoholic stutter
the glass returning to sand

Even the end of the city
with its frostbitten limp
and cocaine
and fugitives
is nodding off

to the music of gunpowder
again

A river of children
falling quiet
at the foot of the bed

John Prine on a Full Moon in April

Lotta candles this week.
Lotta bees in the yard.
Was a time I'd have called
them a plague
but country music plays
better than that now.

Call it a scattered lantern.
Call it the alarm going off,
the rye trying the window,
the elbowed wind arriving
like men from the corps.

Call it the fault of flowers
that they are laid like bricks
in the river.

We sink slowly
into the flood.

You Don't Need to Know Much About Dogs to Tell She's Thoroughbred

You could be alone and not
make a poet of yourself.
You could be enough
like this—
        a river only once, the days faster and faster and
peace, peace, peace
and all that

(your strangeness briefly lit
through a crack in the door).

A buck jumps the fence.
As soon as he sees the dog
he forgets completely
how he got here.

The doe on the other side and I lock eyes.
We are at once broken gods
waiting to see if he remembers
in time.

How Short We Are

"The cause of the differing speed of Earth's spin is unknown, but theories abound:
- *The melting of the glaciers means less weight on the poles*
- *Motions of our planet's inner molten core*
- *Seismic activity*
- *The "Chandler wobble"—the movement of Earth's geographical poles across its surface"*

-Jamie Carter, Forbes Magazine, 2022

This table lasted a year
before the flood carried it home
Now it is a second shorter
wedged in the back of a house above the floodwall
where the boys were born
and measured each day in graphite
against the doorjamb

I return with rain wrapped around my ankles
I return with a valley drowning in heat

Once the hurricane passed we wrote
our names along the highwater mark
shoveled bookshelves through the broken screen

where we stopped growing
and fell back to the river
to count the inches of summer

Every line snagging on the tip of a pencil
that cannot tell apart
the lost time
and the water that carries it away

II
Elegy in Pieces

A Week from which Beauty has been Erased

Days don't make sense so I've been counting showers. There's fewer of them. It's been four showers which I'm told is a week but I've always been distrustful of consensus. Everyone agreed upon the bedroom, the bags of ice and shivering wet embraces, the flowers on the floor. Everyone agrees a week has gone by but it hasn't gone anywhere at all.

Ba'alei Shem

I have only just begun collecting tools.
I want to be an optimist
but my God do I count the minutes impatiently.

Soon you'll go up to bed and the continuous
positive airway pressure
will keep you to your body till morning.

I'll sit here and become personal with grief,
pretend to know the names that unlock death,
that came to you in an orange dream
and blossomed and were taken away.

Our Hands Did Not Shed This Blood, Nor Did Our Eyes See

I am sorry for calling
your illness a gift.

We grow towards the sun:
Your secrecy in partial shade,
the eye turning away from wind

in the soft deep medium
of your ancient pottery.

You imagine a fixed point.
A colony of harmonic constants.
A warm note
stretching back through a cavity of rain
where you trace your breath along the
axillary bloom of your grandmother's dying.

Speak to her palms.
They held your first words.
They are so far away,

softened with voices and immigration,
with the ocean at night

her story is spilling
into the whitening pool
of her eyes

Yesterday I Went Downtown

I walked a blind man to church. He wasn't religious, just hungry. I pointed out flower pots, uneven ground.

He'd been to church. Went every Tuesday. Had trouble getting there sometimes.

I said, *It's a nice day.*

Beautiful day, he said.

He said, *Man, I was gonna go over Southside and stick my foot up someone's ass. But I don't think I'm gonna now. Waste of time.*

And then we were there. For a second, I prayed. Like a man with a door on his shoulders and a list of demands pouring through the funnel between God's blind eye and the trailer park. Or a knot of water and smoke rushing back up to be rain.

Death Dresses

The little girl inside
me grew up,
had kids,
died in your bed
(hysterical).

This town ain't big enough
for the both of us anyway,
the he/him beard and my
little ponies.

I was there as much as I could be
but that's not true.
A face painted with hair
consents to rhinestones at the edge of
someone else's reflection.

They/them cast spells with mascara wands in secrecy,
always had pigtails to play with,
dreamed of being a sniper over cherry pie
and buttercups gathered from wet football fields
in helmets that never fit.

There is no absolute
difference between us.

As a man I've had rites of silence and
boneshackled foresters, blood meridians,
marksmanship,
swimsuit editions.

I had idols with gruff voices, bubblegum cards,
stats, body armor. A battlefield. A legacy of
motorbikes.

Death dresses in silks
and oils lifted from altars by soundless fire,
says the words *Lapis Lazuli*
in reference to maternity,
cracks an egg into cake batter.
She plucks the flame from your candle as though it were a flower,
as though it were a harp string inside a womb.

I have been built to carry bodies.
But who is to say I have the hands for it

In the Afternoon I Will Be Home

I am overwhelmed with ordinariness.
I used to believe all I needed was a cigarette,
I used to get loud at the end of my sentences.

Yesterday we assembled a greenhouse in the rain.
The dog was soft around her ears,
the tea, steeped too long.
There was a television of laughter between us.

You sent me inside early where I fell into things people do when they are doing nothing,

when they can't decide which parts of themselves to forget.

Empty Road Where Someone Is Walking

For all the time we spend remembering ourselves
we might wonder who is left to forget.

Light bends around schooldays,
old music sticks to the windshield,
slapping at raindrops that would fold away the afternoon
before we learned the secret of perfume,
of dancing gently against the night.

I became a man who dropped things in anger,
crushed twenty years under a bootheel.

Behind them turns the mobile
with its animal dreams
marching through the dust of nightlights
in the sweetness of construction paper cut from my palms,
in the vanilla wind of sleep.

I became a man who knew terror,
who ran at every sudden sound
with a weapon.

Life is a circle within a circle
within a circle bound together by time.
I too am a target at the edge of the road.

They honk and I think
how lucky they are
I am not the person
I used to be.

Don't let your cut foot ruin our walk on the beach

Tell me about the cops
who once stood in the stall beside you
at the Southside shooting range
while you painted each other with paper imaginations

Before they dragged you to prison
with all the joy of an old man whose dog came home at last

How every footprint in the south feels like a clue you left behind

There are little embers sharpening on the wind
of a thin blue dusk

racing the tide for a crumpled paper
at the edge of some cutrate Jerusalem

Because Jerusalem Is a Point in My Heart I Have Fallen Asleep With Candles Burning

I believe I am in Gaza
Or maybe Israel
I do not know what to call it
I do not believe
I'll ever return

The streets are gray and hungry with flags
White flags and black flags
Triangles and stars
Made of triangles

A boy with a circle of rivets around his eye
Is crying
When we hug I say *I'm sorry*
When I say I'm sorry
Rain arrives

The rain is a soldier who aims at the ground
I cannot find my coat
Everything is lost

I want to say so much
I say nothing

The streets so full of feet they leave no prints
Our hands disappearing
The way voices do
When they are all speaking at once
Or all at once your own

We Can't Help Ourselves

Your death would make a great song.
Let me help you
down into this cold black android
with the alchemist's tattoo,
the holiday of gunfire.

What have I done but name things
in my own image—
the county's hollowed out line,
the revolution we were too tired to speak through it.

I will call your territories blue,
follow you from door to door,
announce your career to an admiring senate
who will say, *yes, we've admired their economy
of dreams, their precise recipes, their discreet
hunger.*

We can abolish them together,
spell you in ash before the day is out.

Let me drag you through the ink of their suits,
sign my name under the collar of gowns I have sewn
from your tragedy;

your bad day with a hat,
your routine slit behind its ear,
pressed to the road listening

for a pale man with a notebook
to gather up your broken throat,
press it between the pages of a dictionary. Say,
*I'm here to help. Please,
let me. Let me. Let me.*

Generation

An anthem playing through tincans rolling down the empty mall at the bottom of history swells in your chest. A Bavarian motor tapping plateglass darkened with 90s money. Sidewalks smoothed with breakdance, airwalk, calamity. Overseas; rebellion. All around here the doors knock and knock. Every night is a count of bootprints and glass. The ever widening television to conceal us. The vigor of forgetting each story just to discover it again in an idling car full of muted biographies. And oh if we had just stayed in. If we had just quieted a little more. We throw our hands up. To quit. Pray. Surrender. Our heads stretched open by everything that comes through the radio on a shoulder of the blue news recording our names. The queer and the silent. The anarchist running arms to the floor of a womb where something must be born. Breathing or still. Bloodied, bloodied all the same.

Pogroms and Shoahs

The old men were tying *tzitzit* around
the edges of evening.

I remember them smiling
in the gunmetal gray
of mumbled prayer
as though holding something
serrated
between their teeth.

That's how we
were taught to pray—
like we were lacing up the boots
of dead men

learning to laugh.

The Name of Every God Is Surrounded by Loss

These dust storms are the desert itself trying to bury us. They stumble over the dark mile to the temple. Inside the air is still and purple as grief. A bell sounds. A sob escapes the light. It is dawn and people are feeling for the sun in corners they kept for comfort. All at once the birds in your chest are silent. The wind breaks open and inside it is a golden ball shivering to a stop at the bottom of an empty lake. Outside someone lights a cigarette. Prayer shawls rise on the wind, freeing themselves from the same line in every book.

Recipes

Upon Reading "Eminemental: Playing Hip-Hop to Cheese Produces the Funkiest Flavour, Say Scientists" by Will Lavin

In the notebook with the Top Secret gaff tape cover there are four recipes:

Pork Rub 1

Pork Rub 2

Brisket Rub

Death.

Between them are variations of powder and oil I read aloud in the kitchen. They come out red, draped in salt. Like a bugle yelping under the heel of medical terminology. People walk out like children and come back with no hair. Shatter across monologues that can no longer feel the floor. Across sad linoleum like loose change. Like bad theatre. Like a block print of fireworks.

A blue pact of pale dinners, skin conditions, vistas with compromises convenes on Tuesdays (how appropriate) and reconvenes when someone has died. Sometimes there is wine and cheese. *"The cheese aged with Mozart has a relaxed flavor when compared to non-musical cheese. Already people have called requesting cheese that has listened to the blues, Balkan music, and ACDC."* I can no longer comment on the wine.

Last week we had a statue of fire say *Love is the angriest I've ever been.* She worked full time and couldn't afford to drink.

~~The key to a good recipe is C.~~
The key to a good recipe is narrative.
I have one about a highway obstructed by axillary blooms. Subplots of lowing oil rigs, automatic doorways, fatal flaws with lipstick. Bitterness and heat. You've been hearing this your whole life - an alarm swallows a dream. There is turmeric. Ginger. A speech that steps backward like a mirror covered in black cloth. A candle by an open window. A woman with a torch points out a clock stopped between numbers to people you cannot see.

The notebook is lost. There is no secret. If you find it, there's an address on the inside. I'll be in the kitchen at the top of the stairs, setting clocks back without music. Cooking something flavorless. Typing it all out. Every letter on this keyboard is the same.

The Well

They shouted into the well
until their voices didn't come back
and spent their nights staring at each other
like wet black stones
wedged into the corner of the county

One day things will be overflowing
and we won't have to imagine
how the bucket feels when it's full

Or see ourselves through a hole
in someone else's head.

Therin

Who have you been today
A council of wrathful deities
A drunkard with an ark
The fool finally arriving to find himself exactly where he started

You have arranged symphonies of sugar skulls on an altar set with laughter and tapestries
And sadness
You have met ancestors in the wrinkled face of the river
You have been a heron and your call is blue, blue, blue

You were killed in a deep ribbon of California
And your paintings are all scattered and sacred
Over the charted American heart

Your palms were lined twice and now the bright blue light accepts you

What we have lit is a moment breaking with heat

What we remember is not the ghost of your umber
Or the face that disguised you

Here the stars drone at Appalachian angles like a map of the past

You are a highway in the distance
A canvas of mystery
The cup spilling over with silk

The garden of being
Unguarded at last

The Gravel Pits

All night the factory is a hall in the river
All night it manufactures the earth

the other boats leave at dusk and we witness
the distance of creation
witness its endless machine

Love[sic]

Now that panic is thin
And all our errands remind us of what we have
Not forgotten
I grieve you so sweetly

I grieve you along the edges of sleep
I grieve you in tremoring light
In a tarpaulin of blue music
Hanging from the open call of burden and lark

In isopropyl mail I grieve the letters of your name
I grieve the torn package of your voice
Arriving from the state

My grief is a laundry of pulp
Dressed in gymnasium distance
My grief is a star that awakens the tip
Of blackened rope from slouching
A holiday in the window
A gathering at the door

For processions of hungry arrivals
Forming in rain
Let me rush to say I grieve you
Let me pull my boot from this squirming thing
Allow me to say the truth:
That we have lost songs to this conversation
But not an acre of music
Has passed

In overgrown fields ascending
I grieve you
In an arrow of migrant plume
I grieve you
In the ginger and jasmine of rest
I grieve you
In an altar of unnamed saints
I grieve you

I grieve you with the arms
Of a priest
With healers of
Squandered afternoons
I grieve you
With all the sadness
In the treasury of time

I grieve you in a regency of clouds
In a statue of robes
With tongues scraping
The numb empty sky
Where we have met
Only in passing

I grieve your unseen body
In coils of sleep
I grieve your infinite space
I grieve your wheel of breath
That moves the body of light
Through green tangled past
Through the soil of turning stones
Through mugwort of laughter and confusion -
                        I grieve you I grieve you I grieve you

Holy shadow
Sliver of sacred bone
With your flowers and pining
With your swallowing eyes
Your walking still sings in the drum of the earth
Your skin is still stretched over the organism of your ritual
Your vine is still rising from ash in the shell
Where your cards are decided
The morning arrives again
Under the spell of your perfect breath
Your thought meets the wind

There is no secret
Between love and grieving.

Ad Astra

My grandparents lived in Alabama at the end of the old mountains where their grandparents were born. Thin deep rivers wore their emotions on granny's skin. There were centuries of tents arriving to trade with her blood. I am not in line for the pastor. I am not Appalachian.

My grandparents were born in New York. Theirs, in memories of Poland, in jaws of Ukraine, which had the Hebrew lust but did not close around them. The ram's horn is the fugitive music of my grandmother's laughter. I am not Jewish. I am not Baltic around the mouth.

I have spent twenty years circling Richmond. Fanning myself in the empty church of its alleys. Bending my heel to cobblestone. Feeding the canal my complexion. I have put meat on the fire for every traveler on broad street. We become drunk on the water, feel our way to bed in the dark. These songs get in through the floodwall. I have learned all of their names. I am not from Richmond.

A man with many homes has no face.
A man with many faces has no home.
And yet,
says the river, *And yet*

III
The Cailleach

III
The Cailleach

Blood Alluvium

This channel is a genealogy of wounds
where the names of gods were
slaughtered, laid out over the earth,
confused with mountains by their descendants.

On one side the stones hide my family
from the red passage of time—
the weapons it carries,
its decorations on the wall.

On the other, I am a sabbath
of stolen blood arriving
on the smoke of forbidden animals
tearing at the scroll of my veins
in a nation of foreign teeth.

The water between my feet
learns the laughter of history
rushing to the sea.

In the Stillness After Impact

The drumming starts. A train clacks by. A woodpecker earns his name. A bedframe hits the wall. A heart pounds against the fugitive's ribs. The washing machine shifts gears. On the other side of the woods someone is hammering a house together. The faucet drips and after the storm rain keeps falling from the corner. A stick hits every post in the fence. A tire swing is empty and throbs against oak. The grinding of continents comes undone into a series of deep clicks. Scientists have recorded the voice of the universe and it is the sound between impacts. The ringing in our ears slowed to a hooded growl. The extended pant of the dog behind the door, pacing linoleum while squirrels tapdance over the roof and thunder is pulled off the world like a sheet from fitful dreaming. The battlefield of history is a pulse in the earth. All of its guns are alive, suspended in the electric webbing that carries their prose to the haunted root at the bottom of music. All the feet of the city fall into a perfect march that records the pace of everything at once.

There is a pile of stones in the yard. As you approach, the stones become a crow. When it sees what is in your eyes it flies away. You open your mouth and a bird hits the window. Then another. By the time you form a word it is all completely still.

The New Weather

That morning when the first wren parted its beak the song came out in a loose coil. A white wisp unwinding itself into the suede of predawn. And then the finches. The corvids. The cardinals unstitched from the state flag, bobbing faintly in the windless branches of the year. They let out their tiny, frayed threads—muted, dark, felted together in a silent chorus that gathered along ditch barricades and the hollowed banks of the river. Toppling across the roads into town. Whitening gaps in the forest. Swelling through city streets. Every shivering bag on the sidewalk was an animal in disguise. The sun rose and the fog rose with it, the day the new weather arrived. There has been no music since. Just a long line of voiceless birds printing their pale songs on the frozen air.

The Swallows

They have landed in a hundred rusted swingsets
hanging from the sourwood. I'm sure of it.
A creekbed in the back of the year
is tiled with wind.

The night opens to a bloom of sunsoft antler,
to a trainwhistle pulled up from water,

polished and dark and precious
as sap poured over the last golden hour
of stones we have buried around the house

to hold all this in place.

If I arrive
with eyes wide as mushrooms
and scare off the swallows

it is only to fill the sky with paper
where our names were written over
until the tiny folded pages
were entirely black.
Like books exhausted by time.

Cartography of Winter

After the old woman built the mountains to fit her fingers, her hands became the storms that hide above them through the growing time. With them she struck her staff into the stone where her own reflection hardened at the sun, and the earth deepened, and the floods came. Half of the mountains rode into the dark heat of the west. Swamps formed at their feet. Jungles climbed their slopes, teeming with a million battles of rising blood. The first people to arrive spoke the language of the forest. They painted each war with the stars that escaped the canopy. Sang up the sap of every ancient tree that held the memory of the land to the heavens and called down the storms that shaped them.

On the other side she buried her plaids in the ocean and laid down her basket of stones. Weary of the tremoring earth she rested in the valley of her bones, and there came to her a swift dream from which all the grasses and oaks grew upon the island of her breath. The beak that smooths the stone wearing a trough through centuries of sleep, the caves full of music from a timeless world. The people carrying their harvest to the circle of her eye that waits to open on the moonless veil between waking and every story, every air, every family—to this day are born from her tongue that turns from flesh to stone to light and even in sleep has never stopped speaking.

You Don't Steal From the Witch's Garden

This girl has flowers
in her arms,
         ink from Araby,
   embraces like curry
in a burning room,
or a spice market
on its side.

When she
touches you it is
the way children splash
in aspects of autumn, and
marigolds always face you
somehow.

You can be wiped from the corner
of an all-seeing eye.

There is that kind of heat
in some hands.
There is palo santo
and self-immolation
and
no painting is safe.

A Radiology of Time in Garamond

She is imagining herself with a crow on her shoulder,
an eye from the land of the young
growing distant as the sun.

I imagine lawns in Kentucky are blue
and the phone call with heavy drums behind it
is the sound of the shore where we will live
when the gods have been given enough blood.

Just now there are birds muted by a double pane.
They are the color of the south in November,
always moving in the provinces
toward the magnet that beats
in the private metronome of the earth.

They have carried the hedgerow in splinters
pulled from human fault
to borders we laid over the last hours
before dawn broke the lie of history
into our rented house.

She is picturing herself with a family of wings falling around her;
tiny desires tugging at the hem she stitched in another life,
making small wounds that all resemble
in some way
things we have offered the cave
that leads to a candle unshaken by breath

Tír na nÓg

With all the words for this color
I am aging by fire.

The light on the wrong side of the window
a passage tomb in every man's voice.

We walk around with a river inside.
The river is a flag snapping in the youngest mouths
toward the sea.

The taste of soil falls from the ocean
to tired men at the gates of silence
who rifle through our books of fruit and flowers
in the warped chemistry of dawn,

and wait to take the rest from a line of haggard boots
forming at the entrance to the dark metal sky

Now That I Have Met Your Family of Ghosts, I Renounce My Nation

At first I was far away
And had the fear of it.
My strange feet, defenseless.

I would learn to lean on different vowels,
Climb down into the air beneath the country,
Touch my forehead to its backwards sea.

As time went by I would have songs
For the harvest. Milk under the bridge.

With a bellyfull of farmland
And tea pulled up from the charcoal pasture
Of your grandmother's voice
I would make a garden of rain,
Hammer a roof over the marriage.

It would be easier to be one thing—
Tzitzit. Claddagh. A braid of blood
Flying in ancient airs;

A shelter from the American sun
That grew to be so far away

The Sound in This Time of Being

Flames gather without balance from intoxicated ossuary
Pothos tremble against brick
Feral colonies agonize in the black bath of winter
The writhing urban stillness
The winding declawed sirens with chipped ears breaking in
Waves upon seasons of mothdeath and vanishing wings

One flame is a warning
Two is a weapon
Three is a wall

We will climb
Biting the names of every creeping thing
And those that go along the ground
And those we must not kill
Am I my only keeper

My numb white hands mashing the tube of my breath
My panhandle of heat that will not glow
My desperate honesty
My well appointed dormitory ablaze with restless powders and cats
My towering linens
My automatic payments
My bathtub that has never known thirst
My refrigerator whining
My assembly of sacred things
My reflexive television
My constant electric presence an eel licking each night with the voice of un-
reachable fires

My cinnamon broom riding wallpaper through November shedding like a dog
who has been dead all year

My delivery of candles to sunburnt doorways and sugared economic rite
My Amazonian blasphemies
Endangered recreational waste
Hand tufted millstones with runic deceit
Black sage burning redemption

Redeem me I am redeemed
In the digital purr
The sacral taint of secrecy
Detoxifying furnace erupting with jimson and nightshade
The angry oil pocked with recipes recurring

The soft door of birth forgotten
The call of wings to mausoleum oath
The solemn harvest
The thankless feast
The wishbone frosted with clenching disowned paternity
The rigor and doubt dethroned
In flattened calibers
In ballistic admonishment
In unwitting weakness

Six wands with a crown
Six sides of the star
Six equilateral pronouncements
Between atonement and dying

The soft door of dying
The place we must rest in idolatry
Upon the milk-wet mouth of color beneath color
Of soil beneath soil
Of stone beneath stone
Of word beneath word
To be spoken again
As a single unspendable sound.

55

A Map of the Underworld

If you plant dawn redwoods in a line down the center of an avenue they will grow into a map of the underworld.

68 years ago they made blue typewriters with wrinkle paint. This was to show poets who could not afford to fly what the ocean meant to God.

Many grew dizzy with the responsibility of it. Clumsy with the truth. When the paint chips there is nothing you can do to hide the frame chiming through. Every boat crossing an ocean trails a wound. Spoils a secret.

78 years ago ancient trees came back from extinction/China and were planted in Richmond. For a few hours they grew over the Atlantic.

I ride across town with my hermes rocket. In the median treebark peels away from the rush of blood and machinery.

Inside everything is a metal core that changes clothes. Destiny is another word for undressing. The pass between trees is the nakedness of prayer crossing from one world to another without a map.

Now the false stitch you left so your spirit could escape hangs on a needle that drops into spiral grooves where all the voices of the land turn away, pronouncing a name that is the same in every language.

Sain

Cleansing beneath the salt
The light
The smoke

Cleansing the stones gathered
Solemnly above us

Cleansing the broom threaded
With flowers
The thinning yard of innocence
The braiding fallen light

Sacrosanct in the temple of longing
We are consumed
By a mischief of heat
The thickening sky with
Its terrible jeers
The ceiling of impossible
Paint
The ivy of impenetrable floors
Welcoming you home

Cleansing counter-clockwise
We draw down creation
Through ten inverted emanations
In a mischief of heat

Cleansing we do not eat
Cleansing we do not touch
Cleansing we step into the
River of death and repent
For nature's terrible tongue

Cleansing we piece back the star
With brokenness sewn into our names
With brokenness surrendered by
Exiled seraphim
With brokenness in our pronunciation
Of years

Our bodies a cry for cleansing
That has not come

Calling on the light of creation
To forgive us this sadness
This erotic restraint
This earthen catacomb
This fragment of soiled garden

And carry us through the gate

Tell Ourselves Apart

I love you but you are a river inside me
coming apart in salt that disassembled stars.

We wake in the stomach
of a building aching against water.
Every hour of light in the alley
is a pint of blood in the air.

we end in all the places we touch.
we only ever end

Initiation

In the middle of the night I am taken to an island. The figure at the helm does not turn towards me, but every time it speaks an engine of bees rises on the wind. We are pulling a rope of woodsmoke across the sea. In a circle of broken stone there is a hole in the ground. A murmur of robes raises a lantern to the keening pitch of vanished architecture. You must go down into the earth with the cattle and reemerge. As they fit an iron grate to the dirt above and the cow shakes off the dark, I am laughing in an embarrassed way. There is nothing to see. The voice of god is a fountain of heartbeats issuing from the earth. Here there is silence, a wall that moves under October. And then the ocean behind it, scratching with familiar hands. Now the robes are silent. Light flickers and stacks in great halls, galaxies turning on the pin of the island. Temples drift across the moon. I climb back up into an empty parking lot where an old woman dressed entirely in white pushes a shopping cart full of tattered trashbags into the night.

Acknowledgments

A debt of gratitude is owed to many who have helped shape the content and spirit of this collection. I'm afraid a neglect of names is inevitable in the process of honoring them, but I'll do my best to be both brief and reasonably comprehensive.

My deepest appreciation to the following:

To Taylor Byas. *Blood Alluvium* has evolved profoundly over the past few years, a process that was adeptly facilitated by your editorial guidance. It is hugely difficult for a writer to take themselves out of their own perspective, and your insights were invaluable in reorienting my approach, and reigniting the passions necessary to follow it to completion. Thank you.

To my perennial poetic accomplices, Ryan Kent and Mara Eve Robbins. Your encouragement, feedback, and receptiveness to ungentlemanly venting have kept me going. I don't know that I would have believed in my work enough to bring it to print if it were not for the two of you.

To my cosmic twin, Alane Cameron Ford, for initiating me into the good company and practice of Death. Rock on.

To Faith Anne Butler. For lending a hand.

To all the publications that have featured and promoted my writing.

To everyone at Parlyaree Press. You have far exceeded any vaguely formed expectations I might have held for this process. Your editorial insights, commitment to collaborative creativity, and genuine celebration of my work is more than I have ever hoped for in a publisher. I am honored to be part of your gloriously unjaded community and thrilled to call it a home.

To the unnamed dead who live in these pages: I love you. I forgive you. I'm sorry.

And to Maeve, for putting up with my bullshit and loving/supporting/not shooting me in the kneecap anyway, this collection is for you.

Some poems in this collection, or previous versions thereof, have appeared in the following publications:

Water Below - *Free State Review*
A Week from which Beauty has been Erased - **82 Review*
We Don't Have a Grocery Store but We Got Farmer Joe's - *Dead Mule School of Southern Lit*
You Don't Steal from the Witch's Garden - *Atlas + Alice*
What We Could Say with What We Were Given (previously titled *Open Moons*) - *Twyckenham Notes*
Pogroms and Shoahs - *Coffin Bell Journal*
Love[sic] - *Wrongdoing Magazine*
You Don't Need to Know Much About Dogs - *Wrongdoing Magazine*
Death Dresses - *The New Southern Fugitives*
Driving Around Surry County with Drugs in the Car - *Image Journal*, reprinted with permission
The Swallows - *Witches Magazine*
Recipes - *Grimoire*
We Can't Help Ourselves - *Twyckenham Notes*
How Short We Are - *Poetry Bus*
Now That I've Met Your Family of Ghosts, I Renounce My Nation - *The Storms Journal*
Blood Alluvium - *Clarion*
Initiation - *HAD*
Harvest, We Do Not Sleep Alone, Sain, The Sound in This Time of Being, Oceanography - *The Sound in This Time of Being* (limited release, risoprint chapbook), BIGWRK, 2020

PARLYAREE PRESS is an independent publisher of fiction, creative nonfiction, and poetry. We seek writing that challenges the norm, language that exists in the between, and notions of the oft-overlooked. Founded in Atlanta, Georgia in 2023, PARLYAREE PRESS is dedicated to publishing writing that expands, reveals, and interrogates the mainstream. Our books exist in the liminal space between what was and what will be.

The cant of circus performers, freaks, queers, and thespians, Parlyaree is the invented language required to tell the stories of those othered, to keep their secrets, to keep them safe. It is a polyglot of experiences that may only be told in one's own voice. Parlyaree—as a minted language—borrows from what was to create something new.

That is what excites us at Parlyaree Press. Stories that transform; essays that reimagine; poetry that takes us behind the stanza to the core of our being and back again; language that plays as much as it conveys. As with our namesake, Parlyaree Press holds the space between the complex and the mundane, the new and referential, the othered in the everyday.

Writers: tell us your secrets.
Readers: reimagine your worlds.

Printed in the USA
CPSIA information can be obtained
at www.ICGtesting.com
CBHW012046200824
13484CB00014B/340